A Kid's Guide to Drawing America™

How to Draw
Oregon's
Sights and Symbols

Stephanie True Peters

The Rosen Publishing Group's
PowerKids Press™
New York

Published in 2002 by The Rosen Publishing Group, Inc.
29 East 21st Street, New York, NY 10010

First Edition

Editor: Jannell Khu
Book Design: Kim Sonsky
Layout Design: Michael Donnellan

Illustration Credit: Emily Muschinske
Photo Credits: p. 7 © The Everett Collection; p. 8 © Oregon Historical Society CN000466; p. 9 © Oregon Historical Society 103212; pp. 12, 14 © One Mile Up, Incorporated; p. 16 © W. Wayne Lockwood, M.D./CORBIS; p. 18 © Gunter Marx/CORBIS; p. 20 © Joe McDonald/CORBIS; p. 22 © National Geographic; p. 24 © G.E. Kidder Smith/CORBIS; p. 26 © Jan Butchofsky-Houser/CORBIS; p. 28 © Doug Wilson/CORBIS.

Peters, Stephanie True, 1965–
How to draw Oregon's sights and symbols / Stephanie True Peters.
p. cm. — (A kid's guide to drawing America)
Includes index.
Summary: This book explains how to draw some of Oregon's sights and symbols, including the state seal, the official flower, and the Pioneer Courthouse.
  ISBN 0-8239-6093-5
1. Emblems, State—Oregon—Juvenile literature 2. Oregon—In art—Juvenile literature 3. Drawing—Technique—Juvenile literature [1. Emblems, State—Oregon 2. Oregon 3. Drawing—Technique] I. Title II. Series
  2002
  743'.8'99795—dc21

Manufactured in the United State of America

CONTENTS

Let's Draw Oregon

Have you ever tasted a marionberry? If you've eaten a raspberry and a blackberry in the same mouthful, you've come close! These tart berries are grown only in Oregon. Wheat, hazelnuts, apples, pears, onions, and potatoes also are grown there. However, Oregon is better known for its trees than for its crops. Oregon's top industries are lumber, timber, and paper products made from trees. Cardboard, paper, wood chips, and boards are also produced in Oregon. Oregon even grows and sells Christmas trees.

Tourism is a fast-growing industry in this Pacific Northwest state. Visitors can hike in the Cascade Mountains. They can fish in many rivers, lakes, and streams or in the Pacific Ocean. Some rivers flow very fast, and they are ideal for white-water rafting. Tourists can snowboard or ski on Mount Hood, a dormant volcano that last erupted in 1865. Located in southern Oregon, Crater Lake was once a volcano called Mount Mazama. This volcano exploded more than 7,000 years ago. The explosion left a hole almost 5 miles (8 km) wide and 2,000 feet (610 m) deep. Water from rain and melted snow filled the hole to create the seventh-deepest lake in the world! Now people can visit Crater Lake National Park and can see where the volcano once was.

In this book, you will learn how to draw some of Oregon's most interesting sights and symbols. Directions lead you step-by-step through each drawing. New steps are shown in red. The shapes you'll be drawing are simple. The list below shows some of the shapes you will draw.

You will need the following supplies to draw Oregon's sights and symbols:

- A sketch pad
- An eraser
- A number 2 pencil
- A pencil sharpener

These are some of the shapes and drawing terms you need to know to draw Oregon's sights and symbols:

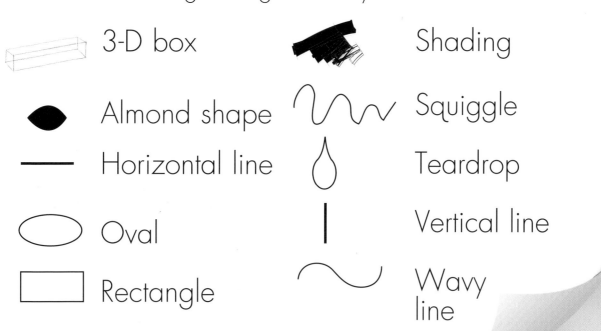

3-D box

Shading

Almond shape

Squiggle

Horizontal line

Teardrop

Oval

Vertical line

Rectangle

Wavy line

The Beaver State

Oregon was once the home of so many beavers it earned the nickname the Beaver State. Beavers added to America's westward expansion. Beaver furs, or pelts, were sold and made into hats and coats. Fur trappers moved farther and farther west to trap the beavers. It wasn't long before settlers heard about the rich land and headed out west. In the nineteenth century, so many beavers were trapped in Oregon that they were almost wiped out. Today beavers are protected in Oregon.

Oregon is the birthplace of Beverly Cleary, the children's book author. She was born in McMinnville, Oregon, on April 12, 1916. Cleary's mother started the town's first lending library! It seemed to Beverly when she was a little girl that most children's books were about polite English children. She decided to write about funny and interesting children, like the friends she grew up with in Portland, Oregon. That's exactly what she did! *Henry Huggins* and *Ramona Forever* are some of her best-known books.

At the Beverly Cleary Sculpture Garden in Grant Park, Portland, Oregon, you can see statues of Henry Huggins, Ramona, and even Ribsy the dog! Beverly Cleary is shown here sitting on Ribsy.

7

Artist in Oregon

Eliza Rosanna Barchus

Although Eliza Rosanna Barchus was born in Utah in 1857, she is known as Oregon's leading nineteenth-century woman painter. The artist settled in Portland when she married John Barchus in 1880. Barchus studied painting while living in Portland.

In 1905, Barchus's paintings were included in the Lewis and Clark Exposition. This was a huge world's fair held in Portland. The exposition honored the 1805 expedition of the Northwest Territory by the famous explorers Lewis and Clark. Barchus won a gold medal at the exposition. Soon after that, postcards were made of her paintings. They were some of the first color postcards ever created.

Barchus was a regionalist painter. Such artists painted landscapes of a particular region in America. In Barchus's case, she painted landscapes of Oregon, California, and Alaska. One of her favorite subjects to paint was Oregon's highest mountain,

Mount Hood. The painting of Mount Hood shown below is a good example of her painting style. It was done in a romantic and very picturesque style.

Barchus was 102 years old when she died in Portland in 1959! Barchus was awarded the title of Oregon Artist by the Oregon state legislature 12 years after her death.

Barchus's favorite landscapes to paint were of mountains. She painted Mt. Hood many times. Mt. Hood is Oregon's highest peak, at 11,239 feet (3,426 m). Barchus painted *Mt. Hood From Lost Lake* circa 1898. It is an oil-on-canvas painting that measures 10" x 12" (25 cm x 30 cm).

Map of Oregon

Map of the Continental United States

Oregon is one of the three Pacific Northwest states. The other two are Washington, which borders Oregon to the north, and Idaho, which borders Oregon to the east. Oregon is divided into western and eastern halves by the Cascade Mountains. Another mountain range, the Coast Range, lies along the west coast of the state. Between these two mountain ranges are forests of cedar, spruce, and fir trees, and rich farmland. Western Oregon is very wet. Some years it rains or snows every day from October to May! To the east of the Cascades, the land is much drier. Two-thirds of eastern Oregon is a high, desert plateau surrounded by mountains. Southeastern Oregon is mainly desert, too, with more small mountains.

1

Draw a rectangle. This is only a guide to help you draw Oregon, so draw lightly and it will be easier to erase later.

2

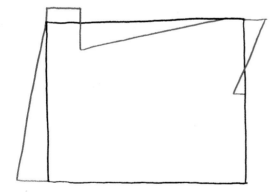

Use the rectangle as a guide to draw the red lines shown above. These lines are also guides.

3

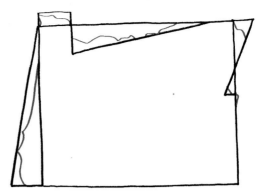

Inside the lines you just drew, draw the borders of the state. Notice that the lines are curvy and wavy. Erase extra lines.

4

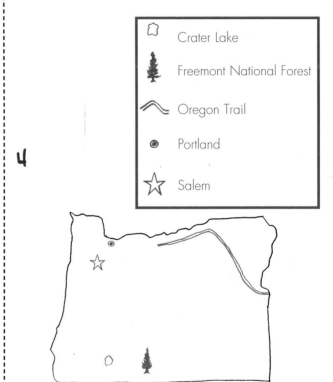

Now let's add some of Oregon's key places:
a. For Crater Lake, draw an open circle.
b. Draw a tree for Freemont National Forest.
c. For the Oregon Trail, draw two lines.
d. Draw a circle with a dot inside for Portland.
e. Draw a star for Salem, the capital city.
If you'd like, you can also draw the map key.

The State Seal

Oregon adopted its state seal in 1859, the year it joined the Union. The shield in the center of the seal shows symbols of Oregon's history. The sheaf of wheat, the plow, and the miner's ax stand for Oregon's industries of farming and mining. The covered wagon represents the settlers who traveled to Oregon in oxen-drawn wagons along the Oregon Trail. There are two ships shown sailing on the Pacific Ocean, one British and one American. The American ship is moving toward Oregon, and the British ship is leaving Oregon. This shows that Oregon was never controlled by a foreign government. The 33 stars show that Oregon became the thirty-third state. The eagle stands for the federal government. The olive branch under the eagle stands for peace, and the arrows stand for military strength.

1

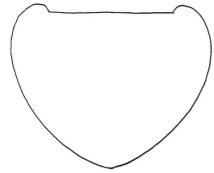

Draw the shape of the shield. It is like a heart with a flat top.

2

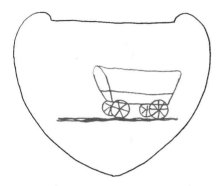

Draw a covered wagon. Draw one shape at a time. If you need help, page 27 has complete instructions on how to draw a covered wagon.

3

Draw two oxen pulling the wagon. Study the oxen carefully before you start.

4

Draw the outline of a mountain on the right side. Now draw a pine tree.

5

On the shield's left side, draw outlines of two ships with sails. Draw a line across the shield beneath the boat for the ocean.

6

Next draw the rising sun.

7

Write the words, "THE UNION." Next draw a plow and a sheaf of wheat.

8

Draw a banner, and add some wavy lines under the boat. You're done!

The State Flag

Oregon adopted its state flag in 1925. Oregon's state flag is unlike any other state's flag, because each side has a different image. One side of the flag has the words "State of Oregon" written on it, along with the date that Oregon joined the Union. Above the date, the flag has the same image and words that are on the state seal. The flag and the seal both have a banner with the words "The Union" written on it. This stands for Oregon's support for the United States. The other side of the flag has a picture of a beaver, Oregon's state animal. The designs on both the state flag and the state seal are in gold on a navy blue field. Navy blue and gold are Oregon's state colors.

1

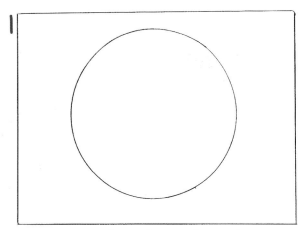

Draw a rectangle and a circle. Make sure these shapes are large enough to fit all the images you will draw.

2

Add another circle inside the first one you drew. You just created a border. Inside the border, write the words "STATE OF OREGON" and the date.

3

Inside the circle, draw a heart shape with a flat top. This is the shield.

4

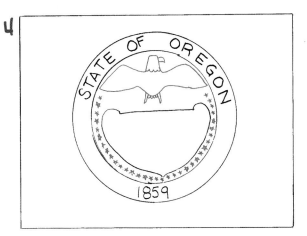

Draw the eagle. Draw its head first, follow with its open wings, and add the details. Now add the stars.

5

Under the eagle, draw the olive branch on the left side and the arrows on the right side.

6

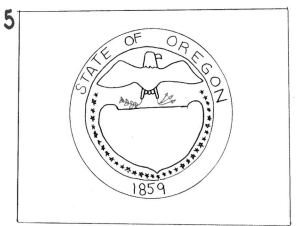

To draw the images inside the shield, refer to the instructions on page 13.

The Oregon Grape

The Oregon grape became Oregon's state flower in 1899. It grows along the Pacific Coast. In 1825, English botanist David Douglas found this plant in what is now Oregon. When he sailed back to England, he took the plant with him. Now the Oregon grape grows in Europe. The Oregon

grape was very useful to pioneers who traveled along the Oregon Trail. They ate the fruit and made a drink from the fruit to cure fevers and soothe upset stomachs. The root of the Oregon grape was also made into medicine. The Oregon grape has waxy green leaves that look like the leaves of holly trees. In the spring, the Oregon grape produces bright yellow, bell-shaped flowers. In the fall, its dark berries ripen. They look like blueberries.

1

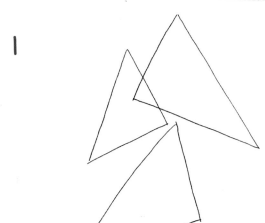

Draw three triangles. The two triangles side by side to the left will be leaves.

5

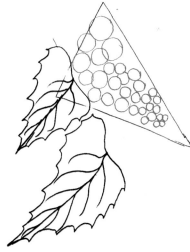

Fill in the area inside the last triangle with different-sized circles. These circles are guides to help you draw the grape flowers.

3

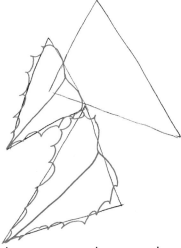

To shape the leaves, copy the curved red lines above and draw a line down the middle of the leaves.

6

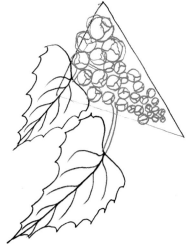

Divide each circle with lines. Notice that the bigger circles are divided with three or four lines. Add stems. Erase extra lines.

4

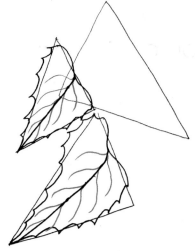

Now draw the veins of the leaves. Erase extra lines.

7

Shade your drawing and you're done.

The Douglas Fir

The Douglas fir became Oregon's state tree in 1939. The tree was named for David Douglas, the same botanist who found the Oregon grape. He found this kind of fir tree in 1826. The Douglas fir grows all over the Northwest. It is a strong, straight evergreen tree with thick bark and soft needles. The Douglas fir can grow to be 200 feet (61 m) tall and can measure 6 feet (2 m) around. The bark is so thick that it can protect the tree from burning during a forest fire! Oregon's lumber industry uses Douglas fir trees' trunks to make boards that are used for buildings. The wood also is used to make cabinets, boxes, and ladders. The Douglas fir is a popular Christmas tree in the United States.

18

1

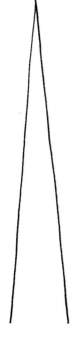

Draw a tall tree trunk.

2

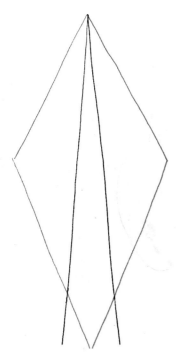

Draw a diamond over the trunk. This will help you fill in the tree's branches.

3

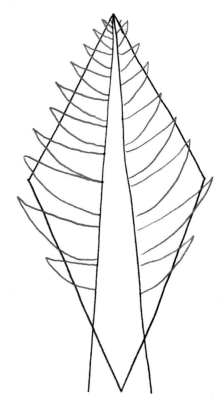

Add the boughs of the tree. Boughs are branches with needles and pinecones. Notice how they curve upward.

4

Draw a line at the base of the trunk. Before you shade the tree, erase extra lines. Shade the tree, and you're done!

19

The Western Meadowlark

In 1927, the Oregon Audubon Society asked Oregon's schoolchildren to pick a state bird. The children voted for the western meadowlark. The western meadowlark became Oregon's state bird that same year. This small bird has yellow feathers with a black *V* shape on its breast. Brown, black, and yellowish feathers cover its back. The western meadowlark builds its nest in small holes in the ground. The nest is shaped like a bowl and is made of grass. The female lays about five eggs. The male likes to perch on fence posts or on trees to sing his beautiful song. The western meadowlark is so popular that Kansas, Nebraska, Montana, North Dakota, and Wyoming also adopted it as their state bird.

1

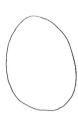

Begin with an oval. This will be the bird's body.

2

Add another oval for the head.

3

Add two half circles for the tops of the legs.

4

Draw a triangle for a pointy beak.

5

Draw two small vertical lines for the neck.

6

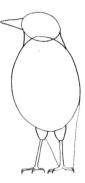

Draw legs, feet, and its tail feathers. Erase extra lines.

7

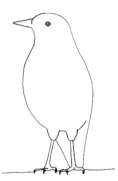

Add a perch for the bird to stand on. Draw a circle for the eye.

8

Shade the bird. Use your pencil to create the look of the feathers. Notice the dark areas on the chest and wings.

The American Beaver

In 1969, the American beaver became Oregon's state animal. Beavers change their environments to make their homes. For example, beavers build dome-shaped homes called lodges. They build lodges in rivers and in streams. They swim in and out of lodges through underwater tunnels. Lodges are built using branches and mud. Beavers are nocturnal, which means that they are active at night. Beavers are comfortable in the water. They have large, webbed feet. They have transparent eyelids, which protect them under the water. They also have waterproof fur. Beavers even have special valves that stop water from entering their nose and ears. Once a year, the female beaver gives birth to several babies, called kits.

1

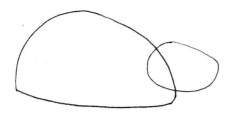

Draw the two shapes above. The bottom of the bigger shape is almost straight.

2

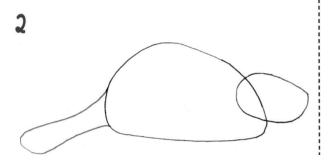

Draw the beaver's tail. The long, flat tail helps the beaver swim.

3

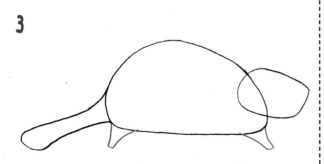

Add two legs. They look almost like triangles.

4

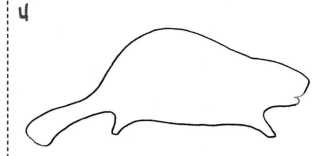

Draw the mouth. After you erase extra lines, your drawing should look like the one above.

5

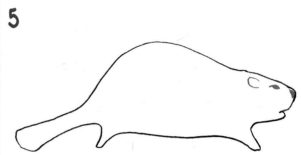

Add the beaver's ear, eye, and nose.

6

To get the look of the beaver's fur, shade some areas darkly and some areas lightly.

The Pioneer Courthouse

The Pioneer Courthouse is located in downtown Portland, Oregon. Construction began in 1869 and ended in 1873. It is the oldest federal building in the Northwest. From 1873 to 1933, it was used as Oregon's federal court. After 1933, it stood empty for a number of years, because it was falling apart. The building was restored in the 1970s, and it is still used as a courthouse.

In 1973, the Pioneer Courthouse was named a National Historic Landmark. This means that it is a protected building and can never be torn down on purpose. In 1993, an earthquake shook the Pacific Northwest, including Portland. Although the Pioneer Courthouse stood firm, it was strengthened in case another, more powerful, earthquake should occur.

1

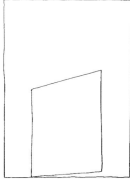

Draw a rectangle. Then draw a smaller rectangle at a slight angle. This angle will result in a side view of the building.

2

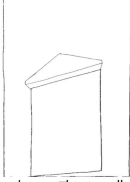

Add a triangle shape. This is called the pediment.

3

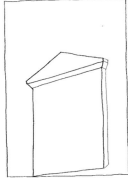

To give the building a 3-D look, draw the red lines as shown above.

4

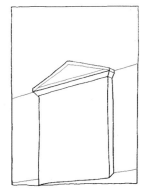

Add another triangle to the pediment. Draw two horizontal lines. Notice their placement.

5

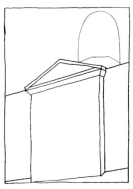

Begin drawing the dome.

6

Add details to the dome. Pay attention to the dome's three sections. Notice that the dome has four main ledges.

7

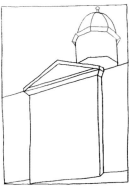

Below the dome's ledge, add three arched windows. Now add windows to the front of the building.

8

Shade and you're done!

25

The Oregon Trail

In the mid-1800s, people traveled along the Oregon Trail to get to the Pacific Northwest. This trail started along the Missouri River and was nearly 2,000 miles (3,219 km) long. Most travelers were headed to western Oregon, where land was ideal for farming. The journey took up to six months. People traveled in covered wagons pulled by oxen or by mules. Many barefoot pioneers had to walk the entire length of the trip alongside their overloaded wagons! Due to the many hardships, 1 of every 10 people died along the way. People stopped using the Oregon Trail when the nation's first transcontinental railroad was completed in 1869. You can still see the ruts, from the wheels of thousands of wagons, along the Oregon Trail.

1

Draw the base of the wagon. Draw the bottom shape first, and work your way up.

2

Draw the front part of the wagon. This will give the wagon a 3-D look. Draw the bottom shape first, and work your way up.

3

Add the wagon's top. It is basically a rectangle. Pay attention to the upper left part of the top, where it curves.

4

Draw the right wheel bigger than the left wheel. Add the hitch, or the part of the wagon that attaches to the horses.

5

Draw the other set of wheels. To draw the man, first study his shape. Then draw his hat and work your way down to his feet. Add his arms. Draw the back of his seat.

6

Begin to draw the horses. Look carefully at the red highlights to get the shapes right. First draw the horse in the foreground. Then draw the horse behind the first one you drew.

7

Add the horses' legs. There are seven visible legs to draw. To draw the hooves, draw a small line across the bottom of each leg. Draw the reins.

8

Shade your drawing. You can also add the grass and the sky.

27

Oregon's Capitol

Salem, Oregon, was chosen as the state capital in 1851. In 1855, the capital was moved to Corvallis, then back to Salem. The first capitol building burned down that same year. In 1876, a second capitol building was completed, but it burned to the ground in 1935! The present capitol was finished in 1938. One of the most important laws passed in this building was the Bottle Bill of 1971. The Bottle Bill stated that all beer and soft-drink containers must be returnable for a refund. The government passed this law to encourage Oregonians to recycle. Before the Bottle Bill was passed, empty bottles made up nearly half of the trash collected along Oregon's roadsides. Now people return their bottles for money instead of tossing them out of their car windows.

1

Draw a square. Add a rectangular door.

2

Add the lines behind the square. Notice the two small horizontal lines that are on the side of the square.

3

Draw the rectangular shape as shown. Notice that the top line is slightly curved.

4

Add a curved line on top of the tallest shape.

5

Draw the statue on top of the curved line you just drew.

6

Draw a rectangle to the left and right of the center part of the building. Now connect the rectangles to the center part of the building.

7

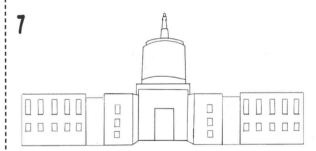

Add two more rectangles on each side of the building. Make note of their shapes and sizes. Now add 26 windows.

8

Add detail and shade.

29

Oregon State Facts

Statehood	February 14, 1859, 33rd state
Area	97,132 square miles (251,571 sq km)
Population	3,421,300
Capital	Salem, population, 122,600
Most Populated City	Portland, population, 480,800
Industries	Timber, paper products, energy, mining
Agriculture	Wheat, Christmas trees, raspberries, blackberries, apples, pears, onions
Nickname	The Beaver State
Motto	She Flies With Her Own Wings
Precious Stone	Sunston
Rock	Thunder egg
Insect	Oregon swallowtail
Animal	Beaver
Bird	Western meadowlark
Nut	Hazelnut
Fish	Chinook salmon
Flower	Oregon grape
Tree	Douglas fir

Glossary

adopted (uh-DOPT-ed) To have accepted or approved something.

agriculture (A-grih-kul-cher) Having to do with farms or farming.

author (AW-thur) A person who writes books, articles, or reports.

botanist (BAH-tun-est) A person who studies flowers.

capital (KA-pih-tul) The place where the government for a certain area is located.

expansion (ek-SPAN-shun) The widening or opening of an area.

federal (FEH-duh-rul) Of the central government.

government (GUH-vern-mint) The people who make laws and run a state or a country.

landmark (LAND-mark) An important building, structure, or place.

legislature (LEH-jihs-lay-cher) A body of people that has the power to make or pass laws.

Northwest Territory (NORTH-west TER-uh-tor-ee) An area of land located west of Pennsylvania. It became part of the United States in 1787.

picturesque (pik-chuh-RESK) Pleasant or interesting to look at.

pioneers (py-uh-NEERZ) Some of the first people to settle in a new area.

plateau (pla-TOH) A flat area of land.

recycle (ree-SY-kl) To save something to be used again instead of throwing it away.

settlers (SEHT-lerz) People who move to a new land to live.

sheaf (SHEEF) A group of grasses or other plants that are bound together.

timber (TIM-bur) Wood that is cut and used for building houses, ships, and other wooden objects.

tourism (TUR-ih-zem) A business that deals with people who travel for pleasure.

transcontinental (tranz-kon-tin-EN-tul) Crossing a continent or a country.

valve (VALV) A device that controls the flow of water from entering spaces.

Index

Web Sites

To find out more about Oregon, check out these Web sites:
http://bluebook.state.or.us
 www.50states.com/oregon.htm